I0371373

Praise for *Let's Pray!*

Dr. Richardson understands the vital need in our day for saints committed to the discipline of prayer. Through this devotional series, we are invited on a journey of growth through prayer and provided with wise and gentle guidance from one who has experienced firsthand the power of a praying community. For anyone seeking to deepen their experience of God and "change the world through prayer," Dr. Richardson provides a practical and valuable resource!

Bill Fiala, PhD, ABPP
Dean of Student Wellness
Office of Student Affairs
Azusa Pacific University

It is with great joy and excitement that I recommend Dr. Elaine Richardson's Let's Pray!

For the well-over thirty years that I have known Dr. Elaine, she has been an exemplary and faithful member of West Angeles Church. She is a dedicated servant of the Lord and her brothers and sisters in Christ. Not content to simply give, she has invested her time and resources in her education and training. She has well-equipped herself to serve by teaching, training, and mentoring all who seek her knowledge of the Bible and living as a productive citizen of the Kingdom of God.

Holding a Doctorate in Psychology in addition to her extensive studies in the Word of God make Dr. Elaine uniquely positioned to offer a wealth of direction and guidance to those who seek to deepen their relationship with God and have a greater impact on the world for the Kingdom of God. She has served for years at West Angeles as one of our Small Group Leaders and works extensively in outreach in the Empowered Women's Ministry and in the Church of God in Christ State Women's Convention.

I'm sure your Christian life will be enhanced and encouraged by the wonderful gems made available here by Dr. Elaine. May you be blessed and Thrive! Let's Pray!

Charles E. Blake, Sr.
Senior Pastor, West Angeles Church
Presiding Bishop Emeritus
Church of God in Christ

LET'S PRAY

LET'S PRAY

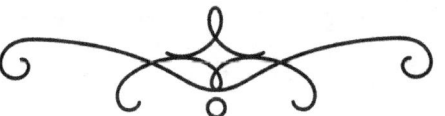

A
16-WEEK PRAYER
DEVOTIONAL

DR. ELAINE RICHARDSON

Tandem Light Press
950 Herrington Rd.
Suite C128
Lawrenceville, GA 30044

Copyright © 2021 by Dr. Elaine Richardson

All rights reserved. No part of this book may be reproduced, scanned, or transmitted in any printed, electronic, mechanical, including photocopying, recording, or any information storage and retrieval system, without permission in writing from the publisher. Please do not participate in or encourage piracy of copyrighted materials in violation of the author's rights.

Tandem Light Press paperback edition Fall 2021

ISBN: 978-1-7376438-5-2
Library of Congress Control Number:

Unless otherwise noted all Biblical passages are from Holy Bible, New International Version®, NIV® Copyright ©1973, 1978, 1984, 2011 by *Biblica, Inc.*® Used by permission. All rights reserved worldwide.

PRINTED IN THE UNITED STATES OF AMERICA

This is dedicated to my grandmothers, my mother, my daughters, aunts and all the women who have poured unceasingly into my life. Without the unconditional love and support I have always received, so much of my life, including this book, would not be possible. Thank you, with love and gratitude.

CONTENTS

Introduction. 1

Week 1: Prayer! Important, Relevant, Effective? Why Pray? 2

Week 2: Expect More! (Self and God) 5

Week 3: Examples of Prayer—Who Prayed and Why? 7

Week 4: Impact—Be an Influencer! 9

Week 5: Who am I? 12

Week 6: Is Anyone Listening?. 15

Week 7: …Even to the Least of Them 18

Week 8: The Mind of Christ—Empowered to Pray 21

Week 9: The Power of Praying Women! 26

Week 10: The Power to Pray Through (Persistence Pays Off) 29

Week 11: The Power of God's Spirit 32

Week 12: Changing Your World Through Prayer! 35

Week 13: Destined to Change 40

Week 14: Renewing Your Mind!. 43

Week 15: The Impact of Transformation! 46

Week 16: Fierce Prayer Warrior! 49

About the Author. 52

INTRODUCTION

Let's Pray began as a Christ centered safe haven created to provide space and opportunity for women to come together to grow and develop in their walk with Christ. Women have been challenged and supported as they received inspiration, confidence, and motivation to achieve their dreams and goals. *Let's Pray* provides the practical application needed to change the everyday woman's relationship to God through prayer.

Our spiritual journey is so personal and important that we often need support that provides perspectives different from our own. *Let's Pray,* will optimally provide challenge and support as readers take advantage the thoughts, discussion questions and opportunities for reflection and application. I am grateful to be a part of your journey.

WEEK 1

Prayer! Important, Relevant, Effective? Why Pray?

SCRIPTURES

Luke 18:1
Ephesians 6:18
James 5:16

REFLECTION

Christians believe prayer is essential. Why? Why is prayer perceived to be such an integral part of the Christian life? To counter life's challenges, a frequent response is "Have you prayed about the situation?" Prayer is a spiritual discipline that connects us to God in a way that promotes and equips us for relationship building. Prayer is the conduit through which believers connect with God, and is spiritual communion with our creator. Our relationship with God is created and sustained by ongoing prayer, which includes thanksgiving, adoration, supplication, and confession. We pray prayers of thanksgiving to express our deep gratitude. We express our adoration for God through prayer. Confession is sometimes difficult for us to articulate as we may not be willing to own our shortcomings. However, confession is one way to clear our hearts prior to supplication. Supplication is where we exercise the ability to petition God for the things we need or want. While prayer is a spiritual discipline, it is also a gift; a gift that continues to give day by day.

DISCUSSION QUESTIONS

1. Is prayer a command or an invitation, or both?
2. How is your prayer life?
3. When do you pray? When challenges or problems arise? Daily? When you remember?

PERSONAL REFLECTION

Consider what you need to cultivate the prayer life you desire.

Week 1

APPLICATION

Start where you are. The spiritual discipline of prayer can be instrumental in your growth and development as a believer. Dedicate specific time this week to connect with God through prayer. If you already have your designated prayer time, consider increasing or having additional time.

What does this mean for me today?

_____

_____

_____

_____

_____

_____

Today I will pray for:

_____

_____

_____

_____

_____

_____

_____

I thank God for my answered prayers:

WEEK 2

Expect More! (Self and God)

SCRIPTURES

James 4:3
Luke 11:5–13
Hebrews 11:6

REFLECTION

Often our expectations meet a low bar. We have low expectations of our own ability to pray an effective prayer. We are sometimes skeptical of God's willingness to respond to our prayers. Our expectations are sometimes based on who we perceive ourselves and God to be. It is important to remember that we have been intentionally created by a loving God who wants the best for us, according to His will and plan. It is also important to remember that we have been invited into relationship with God. We are able to share our thoughts, fears, hopes, and dreams with the One who brought us into existence. We can expect God to be responsive to our earnest, heartfelt prayers.

DISCUSSION QUESTIONS

1. Were you able to have a dedicated time of prayer this past week?
2. What practice has enriched your prayer life?
3. What are your expectations, related to prayer, of yourself? God?
4. What do you think are the benefits and/or value of prayer?

PERSONAL REFLECTION

Spend time this week reflecting on God's responsiveness to your past prayers.

APPLICATION

Practice intercession by praying for others. Journal your response to God in this process.

Let's Pray

What does this mean for me today?

_____

_____

_____

_____

_____

_____

Today I will pray for:

_____

_____

_____

_____

_____

I thank God for my answered prayers:

_____

_____

_____

_____

_____

_____

WEEK 3

Examples of Prayer—Who Prayed and Why?

SCRIPTURES

Psalms 143: 1–David
Matthew 6:9–13–Jesus
Acts 20:36–Paul

REFLECTION

Have you ever felt like you did not know how to pray or what to say? Perhaps you wondered how to start praying. You may feel that you have already prayed often and hard. Wherever you are on your prayer journey, it is beneficial to look to God's Word to see how others before you have entered into conversation with God, and to understand the motivation for prayer. Our scriptures this week explore just a few of those who prayed. When challenged, our prayers may acknowledge our faith and confidence in God to hear us. Jesus himself gave us a model to follow, which acknowledges God's sovereignty, the expectancy of Christ's return, daily provisioning, confession, forgiveness, protection, and honor. The power of prayer is a reflection of the example for us to follow to build the prayer life we aspire to have.

DISCUSSION QUESTIONS

1. What has motivated you to pray this week?
2. Were you able to intercede in prayer on another's behalf?
3. Has following a prayer example been helpful in the past?
4. Do you have a prayer to share with the group?

PERSONAL REFLECTION

Reflect on the variety of prayers found in the Bible.

APPLICATION

Read several prayers and find some (one) that resonate(s) with you and incorporate the prayers into your prayer time.

What does this mean for me today?

_____

_____

_____

_____

_____

Today I will pray for:

_____

_____

_____

_____

I thank God for my answered prayers:

_____

_____

_____

_____

_____

WEEK 4

Impact—Be an Influencer!

SCRIPTURES

Romans 8:26–27
Philippians 4:6–8

REFLECTION

Have your faith journey defined by persistent prayer and bold faith. Prayer is life-changing and impactful. The first life that is changed through prayer is the life of the one who prays. Everything that we need, God is able and willing to provide. Prayer is the way we communicate our hearts to the heart of God. As we pray, we also actively listen for God's response. As your prayer life develops and grows, those in your circle of influence will recognize the positive difference in you. Your prayer life will shape the decisions you make, the places you go, the friends you have, and the things you do. Your prayer life will propel you closer to what God has planned for you to accomplish. An effective prayer life is not a goal but a journey.

DISCUSSION QUESTIONS

1. How is your prayer life now?
2. Who is in your "circle of influence," and how do you impact them?

PERSONAL REFLECTION

Consider how your prayer life has changed over the past four weeks.

APPLICATION

1. Identify and utilize key strategies to positively impact your faith journey and the discipline of prayer.
2. Develop a plan for praying, which specifically includes prayer for others.

What does this mean for me today?

_____

_____

_____

_____

_____

_____

Today I will pray for:

_____

_____

_____

_____

_____

_____

I thank God for my answered prayers:

_____

_____

_____

_____

_____

EMPOWERED TO PRAY!

WEEK 5

Who am I?

PRAYER FOCUS

Family

COMPONENTS OF PRAYER

1. Praise—Praise the Lord! Psalm 150
2. Waiting—Renew their strength Isaiah 40:31
3. Confession—Have mercy on me! Psalm 51:1–10

SCRIPTURE

Psalm 145:2

REFLECTION

A devotional is a short religious service. We embark on this devotional journey for a variety of reasons. Some of which may be community, strength, growth, and development in our prayer lives, or perhaps a closer relationship with God. We all have different reasons why we pray. We pray when we are fearful, or when we want situations and or people to be "different." When we, or our loved ones, are sick, or in crisis, we pray.

Consider your own reasons for praying. Your reasons for praying are rooted in who you are. Your values, beliefs, and, even your biases, have shaped how you pray, when you pray, and even who you pray for. You bring who you are into your family as well as into your community. Who are you? Are you the woman God has created you to be? How do we use today's components of prayer—praise, waiting, and confession—to shape our spiritual identities? Praise helps us to focus and center our thoughts on our Sovereign God. Waiting enables us to hear more clearly from God and sharpens our faith. Waiting also helps us to trust God and His timing. Confession opens the door for self-reflection and leads us to supplication without the burden of our personal failings. May our self-awareness increase, our prayers align with God's heart, and we grow as we are ***empowered to pray!***

DISCUSSION QUESTIONS

1. What has compelled you to pray?
2. What do you value?
3. What are your beliefs?
4. What are your biases?

PERSONAL REFLECTION

This week, reflect on your role, relationships, and impact within your family. Be sure to consider praise, waiting, and confession as you journal your thoughts, feelings, and prayers.

APPLICATION

Allow your reflection to shape your prayers for your family this week. Reconsider relationships and situations that seem beyond your ability to cope. Be intentional about leaving those relationships and situations at the foot of the cross.

What does this mean for me today?

_____

_____

_____

_____

_____

_____

_____

Let's Pray

Today I will pray for:

_____

_____

_____

_____

_____

_____

_____

_____

I thank God for my answered prayers:

_____

_____

_____

_____

_____

_____

_____

_____

_____

WEEK 6

Is Anyone Listening?

PRAYER FOCUS

Our country

COMPONENTS OF PRAYER

- **Read the Word**—Psalm 119:105,11
- **Petition**—2 Thessalonians 1:2–4, 11–12
- **Intercession**—Romans 8:26. Ephesians 1:15–23

SCRIPTURES

1 Peter 4:8 Above all, love each other deeply, because love covers over a multitude of sins.

II Chronicles 7:14 If my people, who are called by my name, will humble themselves and pray and seek my face and turn from their wicked ways, then I will hear from heaven, and I will forgive their sin and will heal their land.

REFLECTION

There is so much being said on every topic; positions and opinions are being ferociously stated. Whether it is social media, online sites, cable news, or private conversations, the chatter is incessant. Is anyone listening or is everyone fighting to be heard? Sometimes, we are tempted to listen and respond to the loudest voices, rather than those voices that speak truth and grace.

The components of prayer, which we discuss this week, create the foundation for us to have thoughtful, appropriate discourse. The heart of prayer is God's Word, which reflects our ability to reach out and God's ability to respond. As Christians, it is important and life-giving to maintain a daily time for reading scripture. To ensure that our petitions are authentic and specific, Jesus has given us a template for prayer, which includes acknowledging God's sovereignty, daily provisioning, forgiveness, protection from evil, and acknowledging God's everlasting power. Pray that your requests will reflect God's will. There are so many reasons to intercede in prayer for others! Especially those who trust you enough to ask you to pray for them. Whether it is fear, weakness, health, resources, family, or any multitude of concerns, you can bring others into God's presence. "I can no longer condemn or hate a brother (sister) for whom I pray, no matter how much trouble he (she) causes me..." Dietrich Bonhoeffer. As you consider everything, remember that you are *empowered to pray!*

DISCUSSION QUESTIONS

1. What voices are important for you to listen to?
2. How are you using your voice? Is anyone listening?
3. Please identify one to two issues that we need to address, as a country. How will this impact your prayer life?

PERSONAL REFLECTION

Use this week to reflect on ways you have presented in conversations in the past and what, if anything, you would change. Also, reflect on the power of your role on those in your circle of influence. Use your journal to write your thoughts, feelings, and prayers.

APPLICATION

Consider the needs of your community, city, state, and country as you pray. Identify specific needs and focus your prayers using this week's components of prayer.

Week 6

What does this mean for me today?

_____

_____

_____

_____

_____

_____

Today I will pray for:

_____

_____

_____

_____

_____

_____

I thank God for my answered prayers:

_____

_____

_____

_____

_____

WEEK 7

…Even to the Least of Them

PRAYER FOCUS

Christians and social justice issues

COMPONENTS OF PRAYER

- **Pray the Word—John 17**
- **Thanksgiving—Philippians 4:6**

  * Be anxious for nothing, but in everything by prayer and supplication, with thanksgiving, let your requests be made known to God;

- **Singing-Psalm 47:6–7**

  * 6 Sing praises to God, sing praises; sing praises to our King, sing praises.
  * 7 For God is the King of all the earth; sing to him a psalm of praise.
  * **Mark 14:26** When they had sung a hymn, they went out to the Mount of Olives.

SCRIPTURES

Matthew 5:43–44 (context fifth chapter)
43 You have heard that it was said, "You shall love your neighbor and hate your enemy."
44 But I say to you, love your enemies, bless those who curse you, do good to those who hate you, and pray for those who spitefully use you and persecute you.

Matthew 25:40, 45 (context Matthew 25:31-46)
40 And the King will answer and say to them, "Assuredly, I say to you, inasmuch as you did *it* to one of the least of these My brethren, you did *it* to Me."

[45] Then He will answer them, saying, "Assuredly, I say to you, inasmuch as you did not do *it* to one of the least of these, you did not do *it* to Me."

REFLECTION

We need God to lead us and guide us as we navigate our world. There are so many challenges confronting us that we cannot successfully overcome them without God's presence and help. When we see and hear of tragedies that come from a hatred of "the other," we must be moved to a compassionate response. Our prayers are hollow if they do not come from a place of grace and mercy. When we pray the Word, we can be assured that we are praying as Jesus prayed. Jesus modeled prayer for us by having prayers that were full of thanksgiving. As we cultivate a dynamic, impactful prayer life, we look to the Psalms for the singing of hymns! To be effective in our prayer life, we must be intentional in our relationship with God and with others. The components of prayer lead us to become ***empowered to pray!***

DISCUSSION QUESTIONS

1. What were you able to pray for this past week? How did God respond to your prayers?
2. How does being a Christian influence your perception of social justice?
3. What social justice challenges would you like to address?
4. What are ***you*** doing to overcome injustice?

PERSONAL REFLECTION

This week, reflect on your role in responding to social injustice from a Christian perspective. Be sure to incorporate praying the Word, thanksgiving, and singing.

APPLICATION

Find a cause and commit it to fervent prayer!

Let's Pray

What does this mean for me today?

_____

_____

_____

_____

_____

_____

Today I will pray for:

_____

_____

_____

_____

_____

I thank God for my answered prayers:

_____

_____

_____

_____

_____

_____

WEEK 8

The Mind of Christ—Empowered to Pray

PRAYER FOCUS

You!

COMPONENTS OF PRAYER

1. **Meditate**

   * **Psalm 119:97–104**
   * **Joshua 1:8–9**

2. **Listen**

   * **2 Corinthians 4:20–21**

3. **Praise**

   * **Psalm 145:2** Every day I will bless You, And I will praise Your name forever and ever.
   * **Acts 16:25** But at midnight Paul and Silas were praying and singing hymns to God, and the prisoners were listening to them.
   * **Hebrew 13:15** Therefore by Him let us continually offer the sacrifice of praise to God, that is, the fruit of *our* lips, giving thanks to His name.

SCRIPTURES

Psalms 51:1–10, 17

REFLECTION

Teach me my need. As we recognize the awareness of our dependence on God, we must first acknowledge God's will and then our own wants and needs. The Mind of Christ is imperative for having a vibrant relationship with God. Anything less leads us to hypocrisy, complacency, and a shallow religious experience. Meditate on God's answered prayers in your life. We must be deeply rooted in God's love and be willing to dwell in His presence to provide space for meditation. Meditation will lead to an openness to hearing from God. As empowered women, are we prepared to have a deep, personal relationship with God? To listen is to hear others and to hear God. Praise is one way to enter into worship! We are invited to offer the sacrifice of praise. Our hearts and minds are transformed by praise. Our prayers are transformed by meditating on God's Word, listening to God, and praising God. With all of the components of prayer and developing the Mind of Christ, we are *empowered to pray!*

DISCUSSION QUESTIONS

1. What was your prayer focus last week?
2. What does our title, "The Mind of Christ" mean to you?
3. Please share some ways you are already embracing "The Mind of Christ."

PERSONAL REFLECTION

Reflect on the twelve components of prayer that we have discussed over the past four weeks.

APPLICATION

Continue to write about your prayer journey and continue to pray as never before.

What does this mean for me today?

_____

_____

_____

_____

_____

Week 8

Today I will pray for:

_____

_____

_____

_____

_____

_____

_____

_____

I thank God for my answered prayers:

_____

_____

_____

_____

_____

_____

_____

_____

THE POWER OF PRAYER

WEEK 9

The Power of Praying Women!

PRAYER FOCUS

Women

SPIRITUAL DISCIPLINE

Service–Mark 10:45 "For even the Son of Man did not come to be served, but to serve, and to give His life a ransom for many."

SCRIPTURES

Judges 4:4–5, 5:1–9
4:5 Now Deborah, a prophetess, the wife of Lapidoth, was judging Israel at that time. ⁵ And she would sit under the palm tree of Deborah between Ramah and Bethel in the mountains of Ephraim. And the children of Israel came up to her for judgment.

Luke 2:36–37
2:36 Now there was one, Anna, a prophetess, the daughter of Phanuel, of the tribe of Asher. She was of a great age, and had lived with a husband seven years from her virginity; ³⁷ and this woman *was* a widow of about eighty-four years, who did not depart from the temple but served *God* with fastings and prayers night and day.

Matthew 15:21–28—The faith of a Canaanite Woman
²⁸ Then Jesus answered and said to her, "O woman, great is your faith! Let it be to you as you desire." And her daughter was healed from that very hour.

REFLECTION

While it is evident that "the prayers of the righteous avails much," we sometimes overlook the specific power of praying women. Women have an immense capacity to see the problems, issues, and concerns of life, which impact them and their loved ones. Women see beyond the bright smiles and cheery facades of those whom they know well. We sometimes do not recognize or acknowledge the power we possess through our relationship with

Jesus Christ. Believing that we lack power is a deception that will relegate us to being mere shadows of the women we are created to be.

Do not allow cultural norms to keep you from praying unceasingly for the issues of life. Do not allow false narratives of who you are to shape your prayer life. Cultivating a powerful prayer life requires personal discipline, which includes developing spiritual disciplines. The spiritual discipline of service allows space for us to accomplish the tasks and routines in our daily lives with joy as we incorporate God's love into all we do. Service can lead us into a place where our hearts can be softened. It is incredibly beneficial for us to remember that service and prayer are inseparable. Let's serve by using *the power of prayer!*

DISCUSSION QUESTIONS

1. What are the indicators of a robust, consistent prayer life?
2. How has the power of prayer been evident in *your* life?
3. How have powerful, praying women impacted your spiritual journey?
4. Share your concept of service as a spiritual discipline.

PERSONAL REFLECTION

This week, reflect on the women in your life and the ways you can positively support them through prayer.

APPLICATION

Utilize the power of prayer to identify opportunities for you to serve others this week.

What does this mean for me today?

_____

_____

_____

_____

_____

Today I will pray for:

_____

_____

_____

_____

_____

I thank God for my answered prayers:

_____

_____

_____

_____

_____

WEEK 10

The Power to Pray Through (Persistence Pays Off)

PRAYER FOCUS

Immovable mountains

SPIRITUAL DISCIPLINE

Fasting—Matthew 17:19–21 [19] Then the disciples came to Jesus privately and said, "Why could we not cast it out?" [20] So Jesus said to them, "Because of your unbelief; for assuredly, I say to you, if you have faith as a mustard seed, you will say to this mountain, 'Move from here to there,' and it will move; and nothing will be impossible for you. [21] However, this kind does not go out except by prayer and fasting."

SCRIPTURES

1 John 5:14–15
[14] Now this is the confidence that we have in Him, that if we ask anything according to His will, He hears us. [15] And if we know that He hears us, whatever we ask, we know that we have the petitions that we have asked of Him.

Psalm 27: 13–14
[13] *I would have lost heart,* unless I had believed that I would see the goodness of the LORD in the land of the living. [14] Wait on the LORD; Be of good courage, and He shall strengthen your heart; Wait, I say, on the LORD!

REFLECTIONS

The power to "pray through" is a concept often spoken of and lived out by older saints. Their example of persistence in prayer has shaped many generations. The good news is that we can all pray through! This quite simply means praying consistently and fervently through any situation. "Praying through" means not giving up or being distracted by time, disappointment, or people. In our *right now* world, we may want to give up when it seems God is not hearing or responding. How often have we been distracted by random thoughts, daydreams, or the next meal? There may be times that we have to acknowledge our boredom, fatigue, and depressive or anxious thoughts. Distractions will come.

One powerful way to help overcome the challenges we face when we pray is to incorporate the spiritual discipline of fasting. Fasting helps clear some of the emotional clutter and shifts our focus from ourselves to God. When we remember that prayer is communication with our creator, the God who loves us, we can prioritize prayer. As we prioritize prayer, our expectation of God is that He will be responsive. With that assurance, we can pray without ceasing. With that assurance, we can pray for the impossible situations of our lives. We can move immoveable mountains by ***the power of prayer!***

DISCUSSION QUESTIONS

1. Were you able to pray for our prayer focus? Please share any challenges or benefits of praying for a specific focus.
2. What opportunities for service did God lead you to over the past week? Were your prayers answered in the way you thought they would be answered?
3. What are the immovable mountains in your life? Are you ready to move them?
4. What challenges are you facing in your prayer life?
5. Which of today's scriptures resonates with you? Why?
6. How can this group support you?

PERSONAL REFLECTION

This week, reflect on ways you have incorporated fasting into your prayer life and identify the benefits, if any, you have experienced.

APPLICATION

Consider an immovable mountain, and commit it to fervent prayer.

Week 10

What does this mean for me today?

_____

_____

_____

_____

_____

_____

_____

Today I will pray for:

_____

_____

_____

_____

_____

I thank God for my answered prayers:

_____

_____

_____

_____

_____

_____

WEEK 11

The Power of God's Spirit

PRAYER FOCUS

God's people

SPIRITUAL DISCIPLINE

Worship—John 4:23–24

23 But the hour is coming, and now is, when the true worshipers will worship the Father in spirit and truth; for the Father is seeking such to worship Him. 24 God *is* Spirit, and those who worship Him must worship in spirit and truth.

SCRIPTURES

Romans 15:13
Now may the God of hope fill you with all joy and peace in believing, that you may abound in hope by the power of the Holy Spirit.
Romans 8:28
Likewise, the Spirit also helps in our weaknesses. For we do not know what we should pray for as we ought, but the Spirit Himself makes intercession for us with groanings which cannot be uttered.

REFLECTIONS

No matter how skilled, prepared, or proficient we may be, there comes a time when we need help. We need help to overcome challenges, to move mountains, and to be just where God would have us be. Our help comes from God. He has prepared a way for us to have all the support we need, to do the work He has given us to do. However, have we put ourselves in a position to receive His help? Putting ourselves in position means seeking and finding God's Spirit. Jesus said He would not leave us comfortless, therefore, the expectation is that believers will accept and welcome God's Spirit into their lives. The impact will be immeasurable.

The core of the phrase "spirit and truth" is worship. Worship is when our spirit connects with God's Spirit. Going to church, singing praise songs, and serving in ministry are all wonderful, but are not worship. Worship occurs when we set aside everything and present our true selves to our living God. When we worship, we can experience *the power of prayer!*

DISCUSSION QUESTIONS

1. How has the perception of the immovable mountains in your life changed?
2. In what ways did fasting prove beneficial this week?
3. How do *you* know you are filled with God's Spirit?
4. In what ways has being filled with God's Spirit impacted your prayer life?

PERSONAL REFLECTION

This week, reflect on the presence of God's Spirit in your life and in the ways you can truly worship God.

APPLICATION

Commit believers everywhere to fervent prayer!

What does this mean for me today?

_____

_____

_____

_____

_____

_____

_____

Let's Pray

Today I will pray for:

_____

_____

_____

_____

_____

_____

_____

I thank God for my answered prayers:

_____

_____

_____

_____

_____

_____

_____

WEEK 12

Changing Your World Through Prayer!

PRAYER FOCUS

Your family, your community, your country, and your world

SPIRITUAL DISCIPLINE

Intercession—1 Timothy 2:1–6 (NIV)

I urge, then, first of all, that petitions, prayers, intercession, and thanksgiving be made for all people— 2 for kings and all those in authority, that we may live peaceful and quiet lives in all godliness and holiness. 3 This is good and pleases God our Savior, 4 who wants all people to be saved and to come to a knowledge of the truth. 5 For there is one God and one mediator between God and mankind, the man Christ Jesus, 6 who gave himself as a ransom for all people.

SCRIPTURES

Romans 8:37

No, in all these things we are more than conquerors through him who loved us.

Ephesians 1:15–21

For this reason, ever since I heard about your faith in the Lord Jesus and your love for all God's people, 16 I have not stopped giving thanks for you, remembering you in my prayers. 17 I keep asking that the God of our Lord Jesus Christ, the glorious Father, may give you the Spirit of wisdom and revelation, so that you may know him better. 18 I pray that the eyes of your heart may be enlightened in order that you may know the hope to which he has called you, the riches of his glorious inheritance in his holy people, 19 and his incomparably great power for us who believe. That power is the same as the mighty strength 20 he exerted when he raised Christ from the dead and seated him at his right hand in the heavenly realms, 21 far above all rule and authority, power and dominion, and every name that is invoked, not only in the present age but also in the one to come.

REFLECTIONS

What does it take to change your world through prayer? Is that a priority for you? Why or why not? Everything we have explored up to this point has led us to a position of recognizing and utilizing our influence; not influence to manipulate others into doing our bidding but using our influence for the sake of the gospel. To affect positive change, we must have a commitment to God, to our mission, and to those whom we impact. Without commitment, we may become distracted, disappointed, and discouraged.

We must also bring awareness of ourselves, people, and situations to our experience. A prayer of intercession is an opportunity to ask God to do what is best in the lives of others. That may be a shift from how we typically pray for people. We often pray for visible needs, which is appropriate; however, praying for God's will to others seems to be the next level. When you enter a space, whether in person or virtually, become aware of who may need your intercession through prayer. When we intercede on behalf of our family, our community, and our world, we can experience *the power of prayer!*

DISCUSSION QUESTIONS

1. How were you able to experience God's presence in a different way over this past week?
2. Has your worship experience been enriched? If so, how?
3. What are some ways you can change *your* world through prayer?
4. What are some obstacles that you may encounter as you intercede for others?
5. Share the impact of this group on your relationship with God?

PERSONAL REFLECTION

This week reflect on the *power of prayer* in your life.

APPLICATION

Bring everything we have covered together as you change your world through prayer.

Week 12

What does this mean for me today?

_____

_____

_____

_____

_____

_____

Today I will pray for:

_____

_____

_____

_____

_____

I thank God for my answered prayers:

_____

_____

_____

_____

_____

TRANSFORMED BY PRAYER

WEEK 13

Destined to Change

PRAYER FOCUS

Our need to be transformed by prayer

SPIRITUAL DISCIPLINE

Confession—John 1:9 If we confess our sins, he is faithful and just and will forgive us our sins and purify us from all unrighteousness.

SCRIPTURES

Romans 12:1–2

[1] Therefore, I urge you, brothers and sisters, in view of God's mercy, to offer your bodies as a living sacrifice, holy and pleasing to God—this is your true and proper worship. [2] Do not conform to the pattern of this world but be transformed by the renewing of your mind. Then you will be able to test and approve what God's will is his good, pleasing, and perfect will.

Colossians 3:12–13

[12] Therefore, as God's chosen people, holy and dearly loved, clothe yourselves with compassion, kindness, humility, gentleness, and patience. [13] Bear with each other and forgive one another if any of you has a grievance against someone. Forgive as the Lord forgave you.

REFLECTION

We are destined to change. One way or another, we will change. However resistant we might be to change, change will happen. Transformation is change. How can we be transformed? Why should we be transformed, and what does it take? These are questions that each person can individually consider. God's Word has the power to impact our thoughts about being transformed. We can move closer to God by renewing our minds, which will impact our thoughts and behavior. One of the key components of transformation is confession. Without acknowledging our sins, we might continue to repeat the behavior that separates us from God. Confession is sincere admission of the sinfulness that is or has been a part of our lives. As we strive toward transformation, let us begin with confession. Once we understand the importance of confession, we are in a greater position to renew our minds. A sure path to renewing your mind is through prayer. Our earnest heartfelt prayer will guide us toward transformation. As we grow, we are **transformed by prayer!**

DISCUSSION QUESTIONS

1. How has the power of prayer been evident in **your** life?
2. How do today's scriptures impact your transformation journey?
3. Share your concept of confession as a spiritual discipline.
4. What discussion questions do you have?

PERSONAL REFLECTION

Read Colossians 3 and reflect on the meaning and implications regarding transformation. Journal your thoughts and feelings about your obstacles to transformation.

APPLICATION

Utilize the power of prayer to identify opportunities for you to confess to God. Ask at least one discussion question based on today's lesson.

What does this mean for me today?

_____

_____

_____

_____

_____

_____

Let's Pray

Today I will pray for:

_____

_____

_____

_____

_____

_____

_____

_____

I thank God for my answered prayers:

_____

_____

_____

_____

_____

_____

_____

_____

WEEK 14

Renewing Your Mind!

PRAYER FOCUS

Believer's transformation by prayer

SPIRITUAL DISCIPLINE

Study—2 Timothy 2:15 Do your best to present yourself to God as one approved by him, a worker who has no need to be ashamed, rightly explaining the word of truth.

SCRIPTURES

Romans 12:1–2

¹ Therefore, I urge you, brothers and sisters, in view of God's mercy, to offer your bodies as a living sacrifice, holy, and pleasing to God—this is your true and proper worship. ² Do not conform to the pattern of this world, but be transformed by the renewing of your mind. Then you will be able to test and approve what God's will is his good, pleasing and perfect will.

Matthew 5:6

Blessed are those who hunger and thirst for righteousness, for they will be filled.

Philippians 4:8

⁸ Finally, brothers and sisters, whatever is true, whatever is noble, whatever is right, whatever is pure, whatever is lovely, whatever is admirable—if anything is excellent or praiseworthy—think about such things.

REFLECTIONS

As with any transformation, there must be reevaluation. Last week, our prayer focus was our need for transformation. Once we have acknowledged our need to be transformed, we create a space for God to move into our hearts and minds. Ideally, we transform into someone who shifts the focus from ourselves to God, His Son, and His Holy Spirit. As our focus shifts, we are encouraged to remember that certain aspects of transformation are important for our success. One relevant aspect of transformation is the concept of character. Character counts! How you live your life, the choices you make, and the ways you navigate your journey are all integral to your character. It is impossible to be transformed without exploration and study. When we commit to studying, we learn and understand God's Word, and the knowledge imparted by his Word. This knowledge will guide us as we seek to renew our minds and become *transformed by prayer!*

DISCUSSION QUESTIONS

1. Were you able to pray for our prayer focus? Please share any challenges or benefits of praying for our need to be transformed by prayer.
2. What obstacles or challenges did you discover as you renewed your mind?
3. What traits would you describe as contributing to your character?
4. How would you describe "hunger and thirst for righteousness?"
5. How have you previously incorporated the spiritual discipline of study?
6. What discussion question do you have?

PERSONAL REFLECTION

This week, reflect on how your character has influenced the ways you are perceived by others. Journal your thoughts and feelings.

APPLICATION

Use this week to increase your study time and journal your progress.

Week 14

What does this mean for me today?

_____

_____

_____

_____

_____

_____

Today I will pray for:

_____

_____

_____

_____

_____

_____

I thank God for my answered prayers:

_____

_____

_____

_____

_____

_____

WEEK 15

The Impact of Transformation!

PRAYER FOCUS

Christians who have lost their way.

SPIRITUAL DISCIPLINE

Gratitude
Psalm 7: 1 I will give thanks to the Lord because of his righteousness; I will sing the praises of the name of the Lord Most High.
1 Thessalonians 5:18 give thanks in all circumstances; for this is God's will for you in Christ Jesus.

SCRIPTURES

John 17 (entire chapter)
17:9 I pray for them. I am not praying for the world, but for those you have given me, for they are yours.
17:20 My prayer is not for them alone. I pray also for those who will believe in me through their message,
Acts 3 1–10

REFLECTIONS

We are being transformed to be different. We cannot remain unchanged in the face of transformative prayer. When we trust God's Word and believe God's Word, we are changed by God's Word. We find prayers throughout the Bible, which guide us in developing an effective prayer life. So, what is the impact of a transformed life? We think differently, we view others differently, and we act differently. Our lens on the world becomes more reflective of a life committed to Christ, rather than a life committed to personal ambitions and gain. When we are transformed by prayer, our focus changes. We begin to seek out opportunities to pray for others or situations. When confronted with challenges—difficult news, hard situations, broken relationships—we are better equipped to pray relentlessly for God's intervention. When we are transformed, prayer becomes essential to our character. The impact of transformation is powerful. Powerful in every way! Use your *power* for good. Change your world through your transformed behavior. Let's be committed to becoming **transformed by prayer!**

DISCUSSION QUESTIONS

1. What did you discover about yourself as you reflected on your character?
2. How has prayer transformed your behavior? Who has been impacted?
3. What is your go-to scripture related to gratitude?

PERSONAL REFLECTION

This week, reflect on your gratitude for the power of transformation by prayer. Consider creating a gratitude journal.

APPLICATION

Incorporate the previous spiritual disciplines as you pray for those who have turned from their relationships with Jesus.

What does this mean for me today?

_____

_____

_____

_____

_____

_____

_____

Let's Pray

Today I will pray for:

_____

_____

_____

_____

_____

_____

_____

_____

I thank God for my answered prayers:

_____

_____

_____

_____

_____

_____

_____

_____

_____

WEEK 16

Fierce Prayer Warrior!

PRAYER FOCUS

Strongholds and unbreakable chains

SPIRITUAL DISCIPLINE

Celebration
Psalm 98:1 Oh, sing to the Lord a new song! For He has done marvelous things;

SCRIPTURES

Romans 8:37 No, in all these things we are more than conquerors through him who loved us.
2 Corinthians 10:3–4
[3] For though we walk in the flesh, we do not war according to the flesh. [4] For the weapons of our warfare *are* not carnal but mighty in God for pulling down strongholds,
Ephesians 6:10–18 The Armor of God

REFLECTIONS

Being transformed by prayer catapults us into a position to be fierce prayer warriors. No matter how we have seen ourselves in the past, we have become empowered women who change the world for Jesus, through prayer. We can do the impossible and the unthinkable through the power of God's Spirit. By knowing God's Word, loving God's Word, and living God's Word, we are able to be examples of righteousness in positive, transformative ways. Our pasts do not determine or limit the scope of our futures. Any limitations we perceive cannot keep us from being who God has intentionally created us to be. As we tear down strongholds and break unbreakable chains, we must celebrate. In the moment, in the here and now, we must celebrate God's power, strength, and His love for each of us. No spiritual victory is complete without celebration. Celebrate being a fierce prayer warrior who has been *transformed by prayer!*

DISCUSSION QUESTIONS

1. Share an impacting scripture from this devotional series.
2. How have you positively changed someone's life?
3. Briefly share a time when you were a "fierce prayer warrior.".
4. Share a brief word of advice with the group.
5. What discussion questions do you have?

REFLECTION

This month reflect on the depth of your growth and power through prayer.

APPLICATION

Pray, journal, and incorporate at least two spiritual disciplines that are not already a part of your prayer life.

What does this mean for me today?

_____

_____

_____

_____

_____

_____

_____

_____

Week 16

Today I will pray for:

_____

_____

_____

_____

_____

_____

_____

_____

I thank God for my answered prayers:

_____

_____

_____

_____

_____

_____

_____

_____

_____

ABOUT THE AUTHOR

Elaine Richardson, Psy.D., has a doctorate in Clinical-Community Psychology. She has been passionate about women's issues, which has been demonstrated in her work academically, clinically, administratively and within ministry. Dr. Richardson has transitioned from a career in higher education to becoming the founder and executive director of the Empowered Women's Ministry which advocates positive support for women's spiritual journey. Dr. Richardson lives in Southern California with her husband, Dr. Greg Richardson, and her family.

www.ingramcontent.com/pod-product-compliance
Lightning Source LLC
Chambersburg PA
CBHW072209100526
44589CB00015B/2443